# Table of Contents

© Frank Schaffer Publications, Inc. 1 FS123254 Skill Drill Grammar Grades 3–4

# Capital Letters Review

## Lesson 1

**Capitalize:**

. . . the first word in every sentence.
. . . the names of people and pets.
. . . the word I.
. . . the names of relatives like Mother and Father when they are used as a name. (When will Mother come home?)
. . . the names of relatives when they are used as a title. (Did Uncle Jim call?)
. . . the first word in the greeting and closing of a letter.

Circle the first letter of each word that should begin with a capital letter.

1. sue is a babysitter.

2. she is going to babysit for aunt irene on monday.

3. cousin billy and cousin corrine are looking forward to her visit.

4. aunt irene moved to culver city, california, in april.

5. to get to her aunt's home, sue takes the bus.

6. she takes the bus at orange grove avenue near grovedale high school.

It's time to review these rules.

7. sue plays with billy and corrine all day.

8. aunt irene asks sue to come again on saturday and sunday.

9. they are going to have a picnic at palm park on saturday.

10. sue will take the children to swim at santa monica beach on sunday.

11. dear sue.

      thank you for watching billy and corrine last week. you did a wonderful job. i hope you can come and help us celebrate independence day in july.

                  love,

                  aunt irene

# Capital Letters Review

Name _____

Date _____

**Capitalize:**

. . . titles of respect like Doctor, Judge, and Miss.
. . . abbreviated titles of respect like Mr., Mrs., Ms., and Dr.
. . . initials that stand for a person's name like Barbara M. Anderson.
    (Put a period after initials.)
. . . the first, last, and important words in titles of books and stories.
. . . the first word in a direct quotation.
. . . the first word in a sentence.
. . . the names of people and places.

*Do you know these rules?*

Circle the first letter of each word that should begin with a capital letter. Put a period after abbreviations.

1. "who read island of the blue dolphins?" asked mr. brown.

2. valerie raised her hand and said, "i finished it last night."

3. mr. brown then said, "the boys and girls who read it will begin reading treasure island."

4. the principal, mrs veirling, walked into the classroom.

5. "i need to see miss francine orloff and miss tammy wynters in my office," said mrs veirling.

6. mrs orloff and mrs wynters were waiting for the girls in the office.

7. "tammy, we are going to see dr. adams," said mrs wynters.

8. "we are flying to see my aunt, professor egan, in virginia," said francine.

9. just then, greg neiman walked into the office.

10. "mr brown would like you to complete your homework for next week," said greg.

3   FS123254 Skill Drill Grammar Grades 3–4

# Periods, Question Marks, and Exclamation Points

## Lesson 3

Name _____

Date _____

- Put a period:

  . . . at the end of a sentence that tells something.
  . . . after abbreviations like Mr., Dr., and Ave.
  . . . after an initial.

- Put a question mark (?) at the end of a sentence that asks a question.
- Put an exclamation point (!) at the end of a sentence that shows strong feeling.

Use periods, question marks, and exclamation points in the right places.

1. Who was knocking at the door.

2. The Yankees won

3. J T spent the summer in Texas

4. Ms Johnson met her friend at Rincon Ave today

5. Your book report is wonderful

6. Dr Jonathon T King was the guest speaker

7. Did your family take a vacation last year

8. Where is Lake Superior located

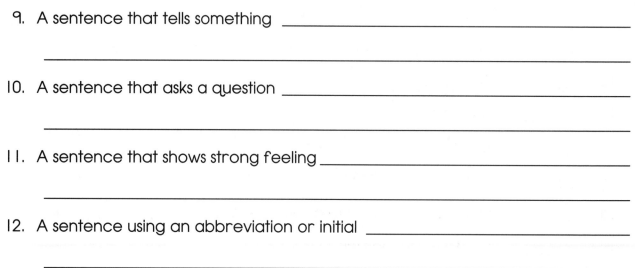

Remember to use periods.

Write your own sentences.

9. A sentence that tells something _____

_____

10. A sentence that asks a question _____

_____

11. A sentence that shows strong feeling _____

_____

12. A sentence using an abbreviation or initial _____

_____

# Sentence Fragments

## Lesson 4

● Sentences are groups of words that tell or ask us something. Sentences are complete thoughts. Groups of words that do not tell or ask us something are called sentence fragments. Fragments are incomplete thoughts.

**Fragment:** The tree's branches

**Sentence:** The tree's branches swayed in the breeze.

Write **S** before each line that is a sentence.
Write **F** before each line that is a fragment.

Does it tell or ask you something?

1. _____ You should know better.

2. _____ Walking faster all the time.

3. _____ Wait outside.

4. _____ Caught the ball and threw it to second base.

5. _____ Every house in town.

6. _____ Sit quietly.

7. _____ They will arrive soon.

8. _____ Close the window.

9. _____ A few people in this club.

10. _____ Today during lunch.

11. _____ He can read well.

12. _____ Swimming against the strong current.

13. _____ Looks like mine.

14. _____ The dog jumped the fence easily.

15. _____ Harold and the other boys on the team.

16. _____ Those girls moved here from Akron.

17. _____ Lou to wash the car.

18. _____ Sally looking out the car window.

# Run-on Sentences

## Lesson 5

Name _____

Date _____

- Sentences are groups of words that tell or ask us something. Run-on sentences are usually made when end punctuation is left out of sentences.

- Begin each sentence with a capital letter.

- Put the right punctuation mark at the end of each sentence.

**Run-on:**
The cat jumped over the fence, it ran across the street.

**Good Sentences:**
The cat jumped over the fence. It ran across the street.

Watch out for run-on sentences.

Write **S** before each line that is a good sentence.
Write **RO** before each line that is a run-on sentence.

1. _____ Jackie and Chris made cookies, they put them in the oven.

2. _____ My friends helped me mow the lawn, soon all the yard work was finished.

3. _____ Julie and I are going to work on our science project all afternoon.

4. _____ Randolph Junior High School is having a beach party, I will go.

5. _____ Ellen and Theresa set the table using their mother's best dishes.

6. _____ Judi shopped for new shoes, there were so many to choose from.

7. _____ The math test was long, I have not done well in math this year.

8. _____ Silvia, would you like to come to my skating party this Saturday morning?

9. _____ In what part of the United States are Lake Erie, Lake Superior, and Lake Huron located?

10. _____ Becky threw the basketball to Alma, she thought it was a good catch.

# Commas

## Lesson 6

- Put a comma after each part of an address.

    Susan traveled east of Omaha, Nebraska, last month.
    Grandfather Adams lives at 1113 Bolton Street, San Francisco, California.

- Put a comma after each part of a date.

    Laurice was born on January 25, 1992, in Los Angeles.

- Do not put a comma after the month if there is no day included in the date.

    I was also born in January 1992.

- Put a comma after the greeting and after the closing in a friendly letter.

    **Greeting:**            **Closing:**
    Dear Francine,           Your friend,
                             Sarah

*I am going to read these rules again!*

Put commas in the right places.

1. Gail attends a special school in Independence Missouri.

2. Her first day of school was October 10 1999.

3. Gail will not have a vacation until December 15 1999.

4. Will she visit her cousin in Jarvis Kentucky in December 1999?

5. Gail will see her grandparents in Blocher Indiana on December 17 1999.

6. On December 21 she will travel to Jarvis Kentucky.

7. Gail's parents live in Canton Ohio.

8. They will see Gail in Canton Ohio on December 24 1999.

9. It sounds as if December 1999 will be a busy time for Gail.

10. Gail wrote a letter to her grandmother in November 1999.

11. Dear Grandma
    I can hardly wait to see you on December 17 1992. May we go shopping after I arrive? I have many gifts to buy. Please send my love to Grandpa.

                                    Love
                                    Gail

# Commas

Lesson 7

- Use commons to separate three or more items in a series.
  Do not use a comma after the last item in the series.

    The boys took a towel, volleyball, and boogie board to the beach.

- **Yes, no, oh,** or **well** should be followed by a comma when used as the first word in a sentence.

    **Yes,** the boys had fun.

- Use a comma or commas to set off the name of a person being spoken to. This is called a noun in direct address.

    **John,** who is going with you?
    Who is going with you, **John**?
    Who, **John,** is going with you?

Put commas in the right places.

1. Doug John and Leo went to the beach.

2. Oh what did they do?

3. They swam ate lunch and played volleyball.

4. Well what did they do with the boogie board?

5. Doug John and Leo took turns using it.

6. Oh how did they use the boogie board?

7. The boys took turn floating paddling and riding the waves on the board.

8. "Leo where are you going?" asked Doug.

9. I'm going to buy hamburgers drinks and fries," said Leo.

10. "Who Leo will go with you?" asked John.

11. "Well would you both come with me?" asked Leo.

12. "Yes we will help you carry the hamburgers fries and drinks," said both boys.

# Word Usage Review

**Lesson 8**

Name _____

Date _____

Should I use to, too, or two?

Fill in each blank with the correct word.

1. "_____ (May, Can) I go to the football game?" asked Allen.

2. "Yes, you _____ (may, can) come, _____," (to, two, too) said Father.

3. They will _____ (let, leave) by _____ (to, two, too) in the afternoon.

4. Allen _____ (sets, sits) in the front seat with his father.

5. "I hope this game is _____ (well, good)," said Father.

6. They drive _____ (to, two, too) the football stadium.

7. "_____ (May, Can) we eat dinner during the game?" asked Allen.

8. "Yes, but we will have to _____ (set, sit) the food on our laps," said Father.

9. They arrive at the stadium and _____ (set, sit) in their seats.

10. "That receiver _____ (may, can) run _____," (well, good) said Allen.

11. The official _____ (let, leave) the Chargers have a time-out.

12. "That was a _____ (well, good) pass!" exclaimed Father.

13. "_____ (May, Can) you pass that _____?" (well, good) asked Allen.

14. "I _____ (may, can) throw a _____ (well, good) pass, but not as _____ (well, good) as he did," said Father.

# Contractions and Double Negatives

**Name** _____

**Date** _____

Lesson 9

- Do not use contractions that end in **n't** with negative words like **no, nothing, no one,** and **never.**

    **Wrong:**
    The girls didn't make **no** cookies.

    **Right:**
    The girls didn't make **any** cookies.

Draw a line under the right word.

1. Brenda isn't bringing **nothing anything.**

2. Father doesn't have **no any** money.

3. They can't seem to find **nothing anything.**

4. We wouldn't do it for just **no one anyone.**

5. Why can't they save **nothing anything?**

6. I can't **never ever** thank you enough.

7. The children didn't waste **no any** time thinking of a new game.

8. Can't **no one anyone** play baseball?

9. I haven't tried **nothing anything** like that.

10. There wasn't **no a** book in sight.

11. Jerry isn't **no a** good swimmer.

It's just like ringing a bell. You're doing swell!

12. The grocery store didn't have **no any** fresh apples.

13. We haven't **never ever** gone to the beach.

14. They aren't doing **nothing anything** special tonight.

15. Isn't **no one anyone** coming to the party tomorrow?

16. Mom isn't planting **no a** vegetable garden this year.

17. My class hasn't had **no any** music lesson for two weeks.

18. There isn't **nothing anything** wrong with the paper.

# Singular and Plural Nouns

Name _____

Date _____

## Lesson 10

That's it! Keep it up!

- A noun is a word that names a person, place, or thing.

  A singular noun names one person, place, or thing.
  A plural noun names more than one person, place, or thing.

- Add **s** to change most singular nouns to plural nouns. **(girl - girls)**

- Add es to a singular noun that ends in sh, ch, s, x, or z to make it plural. **(church - churches)**

- Some singular nouns cannot be changed to plurals by adding **s** or **es.**

Change the following singular nouns to plural nouns.

1. dinosaur _____
2. stone _____
3. ranch _____
4. yard _____
5. baggage _____
6. thermometer _____
7. walrus _____
8. sandwich _____
9. flashlight _____
10. zebra _____
11. glass _____
12. German _____
13. ostrich _____
14. helicopter _____

15. crown _____
16. refrigerator _____
17. turtle _____
18. whisker _____
19. pitcher _____
20. ax _____
21. child _____
22. goose _____
23. cheese _____
24. man _____
25. village _____
26. brush _____
27. thumb _____
28. movie _____

# Singular and Plural Nouns

## Lesson 11

Name _____

Date _____

*Each time you do it right, it gets easier.*

- A noun names a person, place, or thing.

- Vowels are **a, e, i, o,** and **u.**

- Consonants are all the letters of the alphabet except vowels.

    Add **s** to any singular noun ending in **y** after a vowel to make it plural. (**boy - boys** or **key - keys**)

    Changes the y to i and add es to any singular noun ending in y after a consonant. (**lily - lilies** or **fly - flies**)

Change the singular nouns to plural nouns.

1. library _____

2. city _____

3. grocery _____

4. firefly _____

5. boy _____

6. country _____

7. penny _____

8. army _____

9. chimney _____

10. journey _____

11. party _____

12. tray _____

13. company _____

14. pantry _____

15. family _____

16. puppy _____

17. valley _____

18. fairy _____

19. baby _____

20. day _____

21. berry _____

22. navy _____

23. jay _____

24. daisy _____

25. turkey _____

26. derby _____

27. enemy _____

28. toy _____

# Review Test 1

Circle the first letter of each word that should begin with a capital letter.

1. my aunt, mrs. rinckoff, will travel to ireland this year.

2. connie asked, "may i visit grandma on friday?"

3. mr. t. parker has lived in whittier, california, for eleven years.

4. we will be at yellowstone national park on july 4.

5. how long has professor newcomb been gone?

**Think and remember!**

Use periods, question marks, and exclamation points in the right places.

6. The fireworks were great

7. Dr H Berton has his own office

8. Do you know Ms Simpson

Change each sentence fragment to a complete sentence.

9. wearing a red skirt: _____

_____

10. two rabbits and a pony: _____

_____

Put commas in the right places.

11. "Carrie please come here, " said Mother.

12. Yes they moved to Los Angeles California in May 1996.

13. Who ate all the salad pizza and fruit?

Draw a line under the correct word in each sentence.

14. Why can't he have (**no, any**) cake?

15. My sister can run (**good, well**).

16. Please (**sit, set**) beside me.

Change each singular noun to its plural form.

17. lunch _____

18. cherry _____

19. calf _____

20. ray _____

21. dock _____

22. box _____

# Capital Letters

Name _____

Date _____

- Begin the names of countries with capital letters.

    Have you ever been to **Italy**?

- Begin the names of words made from the names of countries with capital letters.

    Is spaghetti an **Italian** food?
    I can speak the **Italian** language.

- Begin the names of nationalities with capital letters. A nationality is the name of a group of people from a particular country or nation.

    Our new neighbors are **Italian.**

Circle the first letter of each word that should begin with a capital letter.

1. The Gabriel family visited asia and europe last year.

2. Their first stop was in china.

3. They found the chinese culture very interesting.

4. Their tour guide helped them with the chinese language.

5. The Gabriels then traveled  to india and on to turkey.

6. Marianne enjoyed the turkish food the best.

7. She didn't enjoy the hot curry the indians used in many of their foods.

8. Barbara used turkish liras to buy a ruffled blouse and skirt.

9. The Gabriels had to exchange their turkish liras for french francs once they arrived in france.

10. They found the french language much easier to understand than chinese.

11. Marianne and Barbara made new friends on their trip through europe.

12. They met a girl and boy from sweden.

13. Ingrid and Kort can speak swedish and english.

14. When the new friends traveled through spain, they all learned a little spanish.

*Some words need a capital letter.*

# Capital Letters

## Lesson 13

Name _____

Date _____

- Capitalize the first, last, and important words in the titles of books, stories, poems, and songs.

  Do not capitalize words like **a, an,** and, **at, by, for, in, of, the, under,** and **with,** unless they are the first word in the title.

Write these titles using capital letters in the right places.

1. there are rocks in my socks _____

2. gus was a friendly ghost _____

3. the book of giant stories _____

4. the teeny, tiny witches _____

5. exploring the world of fossils _____

6. the world of insects _____

7. trilobite, dinosaur, and man _____

8. the art of walt disney _____

9. the life and times of eight presidents _____

10. children around the world _____

11. nature's wonderful family _____

12. the pilgrims and their times _____

13. at the seaside _____

14. to father _____

15. star-spangled banner _____

16. yellow rose of texas _____

17. the new family _____

18. sleeping beauty _____

# Quotation Marks

## Lesson 14

Name _____

Date _____

● Put quotation marks around the titles of songs, poems, and stories.

   Do you know the song "Little Annie Rooney"?

   "Little Annie Rooney" is a funny song.

Circle the first letter of each word that should begin with a capital letter.
Put quotation marks in the right places.

1. One of my favorite poems is called, hearts were made to give away.

2. a room of her own is a very sad story.

3. the stars and stripes forever is a patriotic song.

4. I just learned to play the song blue bells of scotland.

5. Is silent night a Christmas song?

6. My sister just learned to sing twinkle twinkle little star.

7. Rhonda's poem is called bump.

8. making a dirt house was written by A. Hunt.

9. We sang america the beautiful at the assembly.

10. Helen Kronberg wrote the story chad and the toy monkey.

11. Who wrote the story sleeping beauty?

12. paul revere's ride is a historical poem.

13. Is three blind mice a poem or a song?

14. Let's sing home on the range.

Keep up the good work!

# Underlining

Lesson 15

- Book titles are always underlined when handwritten. In when typed, book titles may be underlined or in italics.

    My youngest sister just read the book <u>The Timbertoes.</u>

    <u>Successful American Women</u> is a handy resource book.

Circle the first letter of each word that should begin with a capital letter.
Use underlining in the right places.

1. wishes and christmas wishes is a good holiday book.

2. I just read the book a free nation.

3. american indians is a book of facts about early Native Americans.

4. the frog and the toad was my favorite story in first grade.

5. I liked the name game.

6. fascinating facts was written by D. Louis in 1977.

7. cinderella has been read by many young children.

8. Who wrote little women?

9. Mary's class read me and my little brain.

10. Mrs. Johnson read the mouse and the motorcycle to her class.

11. The tenth grade English class read grapes of wrath.

12. My brother is reading shadow of the bull

It's fun to watch you work!

13. Have you read my friend flicka?

14. Did Jules Verne write 20,000 leagues under the sea?

15. the rule book is in her bookshelf.

16. My dad has an old copy of the hardy boys.

# Quotations
## Lesson 16

- Put quotation marks before and after a direct quotation.
  Direct quotations are the speaker's exact words.

  Mother asked, "Where is Aunt Greta?"

- Do not use quotation marks in an indirect quotation.
  Indirect quotations tell what the speaker said without using the speaker's exact words.

  Mother asked where Aunt Greta had gone.

Write **D.Q.** before each sentence that is a direct quotation.
Write **I.Q.** before each sentence that is an indirect quotation.

Is it a direct quotation or an indirect quotation?

1. _____ Brenda asked to be excused early.

2. _____ Jim shouted, "Look at that horse run!"

3. _____ "What is your name?" asked the teacher.

4. _____ Irene complained that the homework was difficult.

Change each direct quotation to an indirect quotation.

5. "What a wonderful party!" exclaimed Maria.

   _____

6. "Who decorated the walls?" asked Janet.

   _____

7. "Edna and I decorated the entire room," said Roger.

   _____

8. "Edna, will you help me serve the punch?" asked Manuel.

   _____

9. "I would be happy to help," replied Edna.

   _____

# Capital Letters and Quotation Marks

Lesson 17

Begin the first word of a direct quotation with a capital letter.

"My father is a teacher," said Joe.

Joe said, "My father is a teacher."

"My father," said Joe, "is a teacher."

Circle the first letter of each word that should begin with a capital letter.

1. "our class is going to Camp Colby this year," said Mrs. Wurzburg.

2. "when will we go?" asked Zachary.

3. "how long will we be gone?" asked Audrey.

4. "we will drive to Camp Colby on Monday and return on Friday," replied Mrs. Wurzburg.

5. "first," said Mrs. Wurzburg, "we must review the unit on ecology."

6. "write the meaning of the word ecosystem," she said.

7. Mrs. Wurzburg then said, "i would like each of you to complete the vocabulary page for Tuesday."

8. "this is a long list, Bev," said Valerie.

9. Bev asked, "do you have a dictionary at home?"

10. "i have two dictionaries at home," said Valerie.

11. "would you like to borrow one?" asked Valerie.

12. "that would be great!" exclaimed Bev.

13. "today is our big day!" exclaimed Valerie.

14. "did you remember to pack all the items on our list?" asked Bev.

15. "of course," replied Valerie.

It's worth all the effort!

# Quotation Marks
## Lesson 18

Name _____

Date _____

- Put quotation marks before and after a direct quotation.
- Direct quotations are the speaker's exact words.

Notice where the punctuation marks are in the following direct quotations.

"Who is going swimming?" asked Jerome.

Jerome asked, "Who is going swimming?"

"Who," asked Jerome, "is going swimming?"

All of the sentences below contain direct quotations. Put quotation marks where they belong in each sentence.

1. What a hot day! exclaimed Jerome.

2. Sam, would you like to go swimming? he asked.

3. Sam replied, That sounds like a great idea!

4. I need, said Sam, to get my swim trunks and a towel.

5. Let's ride our bicycles to the pond, said Jerome.

6. Do you want to take the short-cut by Mill Park? asked Sam.

7. Jerome replied, I'm not sure that's a good idea.

8. Why not? asked Sam.

9. I've heard that the bridge through Mill Park is unsafe, said Jerome.

10. Well, said Sam, maybe you're right.

11. This looks like a good spot to swim, said Jerome.

12. Okay, said Sam, let's drive in!

13. The water is great! they shouted.

14. Sam said, We'll have to come again tomorrow.

Nothing can stop you once you know how!

# Quotations
## Lesson 19

Remember the rules!

- Use a question mark, exclamation point, or comma to set off the quotation from the rest of the sentence.

- Commas and end punctuation that are part of the quotation belong inside the closing quotation marks.

    "I'll see you tomorrow," said Allison.

    Nora said, "My father will be home any minute."

    "Who," asked Peter, "will win the race?"

Put commas, periods, exclamation points, and question marks in the right places.

1. "What are you reading " asked Mark

2. "I'm reading a book that tells unusual facts " said David

3. David asked "What is the longest river "

4. "I believe it's the Nile River " replied Mark

5. Mark then asked "What birds fly the highest "

6. "According to this book " said David "geese fly the highest "

7. "Did you know that only two types of mammals lay eggs " asked David

8. "I know that one is the duck-billed platypus from Australia " said Mark

9. "What is the other " he asked

10. "The other mammal is the spiny anteater from New Guinea and Australia " replied David

11. "Do spiders live in their webs " asked David

12. "Sure " replied Mark

13. "No, spiders use the webs to catch their food " said David

14. "But there are some spiders that spin special webs under leaves " said Mark

15. "I believe you're right " replied David

# Quotation Marks
## Lesson 20

Name _____

Date _____

- A question mark, exclamation point, or comma is used to set off a direct quotation from the rest of the sentence.

    "Did you call your father?" asked Mr. Dana.

    "Here comes the parade!" shouted George.

    Dorothy said, "Our vacation begins tomorrow."

*Do you know these rules?*

Put question marks, exclamation points, and commas in the right places.

1. "What a delicious chocolate cake " exclaimed Dennis.

2. "Did you bake it " he asked.

3. Jenna replied "Yes, I baked it this morning."

4. "May I try the cake, Jenna " asked Pamela.

5. Jenna replied "You may have a small piece."

6. She continued "I promised to save some for Mom and Dad."

7. Pamela then said "Let's take turns baking something different each day."

8. Dennis said "I'd like to bake chocolate chip cookies."

9. "We can start a baking club " exclaimed Pamela.

10. Jenna said "That sounds good to me."

11. "Dennis, would you like to bake cookies on Wednesday " asked Pamela.

12. "I believe I can be ready by then " answered Dennis.

13. "I would like to make a banana cream pie on Friday " said Jenna.

14. "Would you like to try peach cobbler on Thursday " asked Pamela.

15. "Since we have many desserts " said Dennis "let's try selling the baked goods each day."

# Nouns in Direct Address

## Lesson 21

- A **noun in direct address** is the name or word used to identify a person being spoken to.

    **Ted**, help your brother with the dusting.

    Help your brother with the dusting, **son**.

The noun in direct address in the first sentence is **Ted**.
What is the noun in direct address in the second sentence?
    **Son** is the correct answer.

Underline the noun in direct address in each sentence.

1. Sir, what is the price of this item?

2. What time do you begin your paper route, Larry?

3. The fan, Karen, does not work properly.

4. Jim, have you seen the new computer?

5. We are out of ice, Mom.

6. The principal said, "Come here, young man."

Be patient! You're doing great!

7. Dad, will you help me with my homework?

8. Where, Frank, did you put the basketball?

9. I have completed my assignment, Miss Franklin.

10. What a fine job, son!

11. Dorene, come meet my new neighbor.

12. You are my best friend, Julie.

13. Miss, where is the nearest telephone?

14. When, Coach, will the other team arrive?

15. Mom, Jerry and I would like to see the new movie.

16. Robert, we're going to be late!

17. Mike is here to see you, Dr. Elliott.

18. Mike, will you fix the electric cord?

# Commas and Nouns in Direct Address

Name _____

Date _____

## Lesson 22

- Use a comma or commas to set off a noun in direct address.

  **Ginger**, how tall are you?

  What time is it, **sir**?

  I believe we can do it, **Mike**, if we really try.

You're on your way!

Put commas in the right places.
Underline the noun in direct address in each sentence.

1. "Curtis have you ever eaten octopus?" asked Ralph.

2. "I have only eaten stuffed squid Ralph," replied Curtis.

3. "I have heard that the Japanese eat raw octopus Curtis," remarked Ralph.

4. "I have Ralph heard something similar," said Gloria.

5. "My aunt has eaten cooked snails Gloria," said Vera.

6. "Vera cooked snails are called escargots," said Curtis.

7. "Is that a French name Curtis?" asked Vera.

8. "I believe it is Vera," replied Curtis.

9. "Vera I have tried snake meat," said Gloria.

10. "Have you ever tried frog legs Gloria?" asked Vera.

11. "No, but Jackie has eaten fried frog legs Vera," replied Gloria.

12. Ralph's mother said, "Children it is time for lunch."

13. "What Mother are we having for lunch?" asked Ralph.

14. "Ralph we are having ham sandwiches for lunch," replied Mother.

15. Then she said, "For dessert Ralph we are having chocolate-covered ants!"

# Review Test 2

Name _____

Date _____

Circle the first letter of each word that should begin with a capital letter.

1. "my ancestors came from ireland," said Mary.

2. "the irish people," said Doug, "love to sing happy songs."

3. Irene asked, "do the irish people speak the same language as the scottish?"

Circle the first letter of each word that should begin with a capital letter. Use underlining and quotation marks in the right places.

4. Have you read the book land of the midnight sun?

5. yellow submarine is a great song.

6. We will sing home on the range.

7. Sally titled her story our trip to hawaii.

8. magicians is a book about magic and tricks.

Put quotation marks, commas, and end punctuation in the right places.

9. Are you going to attend summer school asked Kim

10. No said Micky we are going to take a long trip

11. Kim then asked Where will you be going

12. We're driving across the United States answered Micky

13. That sounds exciting exclaimed Kim

Put commas in the right places.

14. Davey do you see the postman yet?

15. I do not Sarah see the postman.

You're going to make it!

16. Will you let me know when he arrives Davey?

# Word Usage: there, their, and they're

Name _____

Date _____

## Lesson 23

- The word **there** is used to mean *in that place, to that place,* or *at that place.*

  The ball rolled over **there**.

- The word **there** is sometimes used with the words **is, are, was,** and **were**.

  **There** are five cookies on the plate.

- The word **their** is used to show ownership or possession.

  The students picked up **their** books.

- The word **they're** is a contraction. It means **they are**.

> You've got a lot of drive!

Fill in the blanks. Use **there, their,** or **they're**.

1.  Nancy and Sue are feeding _____ pets.

2.  _____ feeding the ducks, rabbits, and geese first.

3.  "Nancy, would you carry this bag of food over _____ ?" asked Sue.

4.  "I will carry it over _____ if you will watch that the rabbits

    don't run out of _____ cage," said Sue.

5.  "_____ gone!" shouted Nancy.

6.  The girls looked and saw _____ pet rabbits running off behind the bushes.

7.  "_____ they are!" exclaimed Sue.

8.  Nancy and Sue caught _____ rabbits and put them in

    _____ cage.

9.  _____ now going into the house to feed

    _____ fish.

10. "At least the fish can't swim out of _____ aquarium!" exclaimed Nancy.

© Frank Schaffer Publications, Inc.

FS123254 Skill Drill Grammar

# Word Usage: off and of

## Lesson 24

Name _____

Date _____

Write the correct word.

- The word **of** is used to mean *belonging to something, containing something,* or *about something.*

    May I have a cup **of** milk?

- Do not use the word **of** instead of **have**. Use **have** with the words **ought, must, might,** and **could**.

    **Wrong:** He could of told me.
    **Right:** He could have told me.

- The word **off** is used to mean *away from* or *not on or touching something.*

    The dress was **off** its hanger.

- Do not use the word **off** instead of **from**.

    **Wrong:** Helen borrowed some sugar **off** her neighbor.
    **Right:** Helen borrowed some sugar **from** her neighbor.

- Do not use the word **off** with the word **of.**

Fill in the blanks.

1. May I borrow a piece _____ your paper? **(of, off)**

2. Please take your feet _____ the table. **(off, off of)**

3. Fred borrowed some money _____ his friend. **(off, from)**

4. I ought to _____ finished my homework. **(of, have)**

5. Jeanette must _____ been swimming this afternoon. **(of, have)**

6. "Don't jump _____ the roof!" shouted Mr. Tanza. **(off, off of)**

7. I got some pencils _____ my sister. **(off, off of, from)**

8. That cup _____ cocoa tasted great! **(of, off)**

# Nouns

## Lesson 25

Name _____

Date _____

- A **noun** is a word that names a person, place, or thing.

    Lorenzo plays on a soccer team in Los Angeles.

    Lorenzo names a **person**.
    Los Angeles names a **place**.
    Team names a **thing**.

Does it name a person, place, or thing?

Underline the noun(s) in each sentence.

1. Soccer has become a popular sport in this country.

2. Lorenzo wants to play professional soccer someday.

3. Lorenzo would like to play for the Aztecs.

4. The Aztecs are a professional soccer team in Los Angeles.

5. Lorenzo plays soccer with the Walnut Chargers.

6. Most of his friends play on the same team.

7. The Chargers are tied for the league championship this year.

8. Lorenzo is sure his team will win the title.

Write your own sentences. Underline the nouns in each of your sentences.

9. _____

10. _____

11. _____

12. _____

13. _____

14. _____

15. _____

16. _____

# Nouns and Pronouns

## Lesson 26

- A **noun** is a word that names a person, place, or thing.

- A **pronoun** is a word that takes the place of a noun.
  The most common pronouns are: **I, my, mine, me, he, his, him, she, her, hers, it, its, we, our, ours, us, you, your, yours, they, their, theirs,** and **them.**

Underline the nouns.
Circle the pronouns.

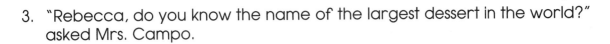

1. Rebecca and her class are studying Africa.

2. Almost half of it is dry, barren dessert.

3. "Rebecca, do you know the name of the largest dessert in the world?" asked Mrs. Campo.

4. "I believe it is the Sahara Desert," answered Rebecca.

5. "It also has grasslands and rain forests," said her teacher.

6. "Are they in the central part of Africa, near the equator?" asked Mike.

7. "You are correct, Mike," said Mrs. Campo.

8. Then she said, "Many of the poor farmers live in mud huts or tents."

9. "Do any Africans live in modern buildings like we have in our country?" asked Patsy.

10. "Yes, they do," replied Mrs. Campo.

11. "Their country sounds very different from ours," remarked Rebecca.

12. "That's right, but we can learn a great deal from their country," replied Mrs. Campo.

13. "What part of the world will we study next?" asked Jim.

14. "Our class will begin to study Asia next week," she answered.

# Singular and Plural Nouns

## Lesson 27

*Do you know these rules?*

- A noun is a word that names a person, place, or thing.

  A singular noun is a word that names one person, place, or thing.
  A plural noun is a word that names more than one person, place, or thing.

  Add **s** to any singular noun ending in **o** after a vowel to make it plural:
  **rodeo - rodeos.**

  Add **es** to any singular noun ending in **o** after a consonant to make it plural:
  **tomato - tomatoes.**
  Words that refer to music are an exception: **piano - pianos.**

Change the following singular nouns to plural nouns. Review the rules in Lessons 10 and 11.

1. wood _____

2. shutter _____

3. church _____

4. lasso _____

5. rocket _____

6. salary _____

7. hero _____

8. glove _____

9. leaf _____

10. box _____

11. bicycle _____

12. journey _____

13. volcano _____

14. suit _____

15. mosquito _____

16. berry _____

17. mouse _____

18. vacation _____

19. lady _____

20. puzzle _____

21. calf _____

22. potato _____

23. woman _____

24. drum _____

25. army _____

26. dress _____

27. zero _____

28. solo _____

29. insect _____

30. loaf _____

# Singular Possessive Nouns

## Lesson 28

- To make a singular noun show possession or ownership, add an **apostrophe** and an **s**.

> It's just like ringing a bell. You're doing swell!

| | |
|---|---|
| Mary - Mary's | Mary's friends are coming soon. |
| town - town's | The town's streets are unpaved. |
| cup - cup's | The cup's handle is broken. |

Change each singular noun to its possessive form.

1. television _____
2. parade _____
3. barber _____
4. hammer _____
5. sweater _____
6. child _____
7. spider _____
8. zipper _____
9. grasshopper _____
10. station _____
11. knife _____
12. country _____
13. piano _____
14. snack _____
15. newspaper _____
16. elephant _____
17. kite _____
18. nest _____

19. crayon _____
20. toe _____
21. lion _____
22. rock _____
23. woman _____
24. dish _____
25. wagon _____
26. bubble _____
27. office _____
28. donkey _____
29. hall _____
30. violin _____
31. potato _____
32. wheel _____
33. yoyo _____
34. moon _____
35. friend _____
36. truck _____

# Plural Possessive Nouns

Lesson 29

- To make a plural noun ending in **s** show possession or ownership, add an **apostrophe after the s.**

    flags - flags'       The flags' colors looked like rainbows.

    calves - calves'     The calves' mother wandered off.

- If a plural noun does not end in **s**, add an apostrophe and an **s** as you would for a singular noun.

    men - men**'s**       The men's clothing is on the second floor.

Change each plural noun to its possessive form.

1. kittens _____
2. brooms _____
3. owls _____
4. children _____
5. lunches _____
6. bells _____
7. farms _____
8. enemies _____
9. pianos _____
10. leaves _____
11. men _____
12. nurses _____
13. homes _____
14. roses _____
15. friends _____
16. parties _____
17. axes _____
18. wolves _____

19. lips _____
20. cups _____
21. doors _____
22. flies _____
23. bridges _____
24. wharves _____
25. seeds _____
26. boxes _____
27. puppies _____
28. armies _____
29. feathers _____
30. trays _____
31. mice _____
32. dentists _____
33. wines _____
34. feet _____
35. hats _____
36. hammers _____

# Common and Proper Nouns

Name _____

Date _____

Lesson 30

- A **common noun** is a word that names **any** person, place, or thing. Words like **river, country, boy, girl, cat, house,** and **school** are common nouns. Common nouns do not begin with a capital letter unless they are the first word of a sentence.

- A **proper noun** is a word that names a **special** person, place, or thing. Words like **Ohio River, Mexico, Danny, Amy, Fluff,** and **Starbuck School** are proper nouns. Proper nouns begin with a capital letter.

Circle each common noun.
Underline each proper noun.

Each time you do it right, it gets easier.

1. My sister traveled to England last August.

2. Mr. Ching is the principal at Olive School.

3. Ken, who is your favorite baseball player?

4. The Dallas Cowboys are great!

5. Canada is north of the United States of America.

6. Mrs. Noce lives in the yellow house on Lanigon Street.

7. What's your favorite food?

8. Sandy must study for her exam in English.

9. Tony and I went fishing yesterday.

10. Our basketball team, the Raiders, is undefeated.

11. Mr. and Mrs. Thatcher moved to Daytona Beach.

12. Does the President of the United States live in the White House?

13. Gilda and Goldie are my pet goldfish.

14. Greg took a walk through Penn Park on Saturday.

15. Our flight to Kentucky will take three hours.

# Common and Proper Nouns

**Name** _____

**Date** _____

Lesson 31

- A common noun is a word that names any person, place, or thing.
  Do not begin a common noun with a capital letter.

- A proper noun is a word that names a special person, place, or thing.
  Begin each proper noun with a capital letter.

Change the proper nouns to common nouns. The first one has been done for you.

1. California  _state_____

2. Mr. Johnson _____

3. Thanksgiving _____

4. Russia _____

5. Idaho _____

6. Memorial Day _____

7. Sacramento _____

8. Mrs. Randal _____

9. Wednesday _____

10. Laura _____

11. Fido _____

12. Monday _____

13. Ben _____

14. First Avenue _____

15. January _____

16. Tammy _____

17. Egypt _____

18. Harvard College _____

19. P.J. Ellis _____

20. Kansas _____

Change the common nouns to proper nouns.

21. holiday _____

22. day _____

23. river _____

24. man _____

25. month _____

26. street _____

27. girl _____

28. country _____

29. city _____

30. school _____

31. pet _____

# Sentence Fragments

## Lesson 32

Name _____

Date _____

● Sentences are groups of words that tell or ask us something. Groups of words that do not tell or ask us something are called sentence fragments.

**Fragment:**
the blue cup

**Complete Sentence:**
Randy drank cocoa from the blue cup.

Change each of the sentence fragments to complete sentences. You may use the fragments at the beginning, middle, or end of your sentences. Use capital letters and punctuation marks in the right places.

1. My wrist watch: _____

   _____

2. apples, oranges, and bananas: _____

   _____

3. Mr. Bamberger's dog: _____

   _____

4. two pencils and a ruler: _____

   _____

5. came in the front door: _____

   _____

6. Billy, Sandra, and Janey: _____

   _____

7. Mother and Father: _____

   _____

8. likes to skate: _____

   _____

# Run-on Sentences

## Lesson 33

Remember to use capital letters and end punctuation.

- Sentences are groups of words that tell or ask us something. Run-on sentences usually occur when end punctuation is left out of sentences. Always remember to put end punctuation at the end of each sentence.

  **Run-on Sentence:**
  It was Dana's turn to bat she hit a home run what a sight!

  **Good Sentence:**
  It was Dana's turn to bat. She hit a home run. What a sight!

Read the short story below. Some beginning capital letters and all end punctuation marks have been left out. Circle the first letter of each word that should begin with a capital letter. Put in end punctuation marks.

### "The School Play"

Katie and her friends want to be in the school play and the try-outs are this afternoon Katie wants to play the lead part so does her friend, Nancy the girls stand on stage and read their lines Nancy thought she read her lines well it is Katie's turn how did she do Katie thought she also read well the girls won't know who won the part until Friday

the big day has finally arrived today is Friday Katie and Nancy walk to the bulletin board both girls really want to win the part they both looked at the same time Barbara Gesto got the part they were very disappointed then they looked again both girls had other parts in the play Nancy and Katie were happy, indeed

# Review Test 3

Fill in the blanks.

1. The lamp belongs over _____ . **(there, their, they're)**

2. Get your feet _____ the table. **(of, off, off of)**

3. _____ my best friends. **(There, Their, They're)**

4. They moved into _____ new house. **(there, their, they're)**

5. He must _____ broken the record. **(of, have)**

6. I received a gift _____ my sister. **(off, from)**

Underline each noun. Circle each pronoun.

7. My family and I moved to Alabama.

8. We are shopping for shoes today.

9. Karen walked to her grandmother's house.

Nothing can stop you once you know how!

Change the proper nouns to common nouns.

10. Africa _____    11. Memorial Day _____

Change the common nouns to proper nouns.

12. lake _____    13. boy _____

Change the following singular and plural nouns to their possessive forms.

14. child _____    15. houses _____

16. man _____    17. tree _____

18. books _____    19. women _____

Write **S** before each line that is a sentence.
Write **F** before each line that is a fragment.
Write **RO** before each line that is a run-on.

20. _____ Tracy played with Mary, they had fun.

21. _____ He threw the ball.

22. _____ The timid cat.

# Verbs

Lesson 34

Name _____

Date _____

- A **verb** is a word that shows action. It shows what someone or something does, did, or will do.

  Grandmother and I **baked** a cake.

  Cheryl **plays** softball every afternoon.

Draw two lines under each verb.

Be patient! You're doing great!

1.  Julie answered the telephone.
2.  Victor and Kevin jumped over the hedge.
3.  Olga asked for another book.
4.  Patty mailed the letters for her mother.
5.  The dogs barked all night.
6.  Our school band marched in the parade.
7.  Mother and Father ate breakfast in bed.
8.  Hundreds of bees buzzed near the hive.
9.  Grandma kissed Jenny on the forehead.
10. Our troop camped near June Lake.
11. The moving men packed all our belongings in the van.
12. The policemen chased the robbers through town.
13. Mr. Kelly read the newspaper in his office.
14. Father and I emptied the shelves.
15. The grasshoppers hopped through the dry wheat fields.
16. Our family vacationed in Mexico last year.
17. Tom whistled for his dog.
18. Lucy shut the shutters.
19. Our dog scratched the fleas behind the ears.
20. Mrs. Taylor pulled weeds from the vegetable garden.

# Helping Verbs

## Lesson 35

Name _____

Date _____

- A verb is a word that shows action.
- Some verbs are used alone.

    Kathy set the table.

- Sometimes a sentence needs more than one verb to make the statement clear. These words are called **helping verbs.**

| Common Helping Verbs | | |
|---|---|---|
| am | were | has |
| are | do | had |
| is | did | can |
| was | have | may |

Each of the sentences below contain a verb and a helping verb.
Draw two lines under the verb and the helping verb.

1. Nick has delivered all the newspapers.

2. The builders were building the building.

3. Who was knocking on the door?

4. My parents are leaving for work at eight o'clock.

5. Father is cooking dinner tonight.

6. The elephants have eaten all the peanuts.

7. Harry can swim well.

8. I am sewing a pair of jeans.

9. Willie may walk to the beach with you.

10. The packages have arrived safely.

11. Frank did complete his assignment.

12. The children do answer the telephone politely.

13. Irene has thrown the ball three times.

14. Mother is working today.

It's worth all the effort!

# Linking Verbs

## Lesson 36

- All verbs help make a statement. Most verbs help make a statement by showing action.

    Jack cooked dinner.

- Other verbs, however, help show the appearance or condition of something. These verbs are called **linking verbs.**

    Her dress **is** lovely.

The most common linking verb is the word **be.** Words like **am, is, are, was, were, being,** and **been** are different forms of the word be. Other common linking verbs are **seem, become, appear, remain, look,** and **feel.**

Draw two lines under the verb in each sentence.

1. Who was the guest speaker?

2. Jenny and I are the only girls on the team.

3. I am the tallest student in my school.

4. Jackie became our new class president.

5. Henry and Larry Conners were in Europe for two weeks.

6. Ms. Bennington is our new principal.

7. The horses appear frightened.

8. The children remained in the house during the thunderstorm.

9. Gilbert looked handsome in his new shirt.

10. Mary seems cold.

11. Who is that girl?

12. Where are the children?

13. I am the new spelling champion.

14. Frankie and Gary were there two years ago.

Keep up the good work!

# Nouns and Verbs

## Lesson 37

**Name** _____

**Date** _____

- A noun is a word that names a person, place, or thing.

    The **children** walked to the pond.

- Proper nouns name special persons, places, or things. Capitalize proper nouns.

    **Michelle** and **Pete** walked to the pond.

- A verb is a word that helps make a statement. It can show action or help show the appearance or condition of something.

    The children **walked** to the pond.

    Each child **is** five years old.

Some sentences use helping verbs.

    The children **are walking** to the pond.

You've got a lot of drive!

Circle each noun.
Draw two lines under each verb.

1. Irene and Melissa are going to the department store.

2. The apples in the supermarket looked fresh.

3. My friend, David, attends Manchester Junior High School.

4. Fluff is chasing the butterfly.

5. Sandy remained for both movies.

6. Ira feels rotten.

7. Dorene toasted marshmallows over the campfire.

8. Marianne has planned a wonderful party.

9. Erin seemed disappointed.

10. Maggie and Lisa had sore feet after the parade.

11. Pete and Josh are going home today.

12. Uncle John caught three fish.

# Subjects and Predicates

**Lesson 38**

Name _____

Date _____

- A sentence is a group of words that tells or asks something.

- Every sentence has two parts: the **subject** and the **predicate**.
The **subject** is what or who is being talked about. The **predicate** is the part that says something about the subject.

   My friend, Glenda, babysits every Saturday.

**Complete Subject:** My friend, Glenda,

**Complete Predicate:** babysits every Saturday.

Draw one line under the complete subject. Draw two lines under the complete predicate.

1. The hunter shot the rabbit.

2. The two groups of children played games.

3. Carrie is ironing shirts in the laundry room.

4. The fierce dog barked at Mr. Plummer.

5. My sister doesn't like baseball.

6. Leslie wrote a letter to her father.

7. The boys were invited to the party.

You're off like a shot!

8. Mrs. Kemper excused Adam from the test.

9. David forgot his books.

10. Vera and Yolanda take the flag down every afternoon.

11. Meg, Amy, and Beth are characters in this story.

12. Lloyd keeps his pet snakes in a cage.

13. Father played checkers with the boys under the tree.

14. Tony watched the television late last night.

15. Mom, Dad, and I went fishing early this morning.

# Subjects and Predicates

## Lesson 39

Name _____

Date _____

- Every sentence has two parts: the subject and the predicate.
  The subject is what or who is being talked about. The predicate is the part that says something about the subject.

  Susan visited Joey and Ted on Friday.

  **Complete Subject:** Susan

  **Complete Predicate:** visited Joey and Ted on Friday.

  *It's fun to watch you work!*

Each subject below needs a predicate. Complete each sentence.
Add end punctuation.

1. Spiders and ants _____

2. That old apple tree _____

3. My brother and I _____

4. The two boxes _____

5. The Jones family _____

6. That new sweater _____

7. An airplane _____

8. My favorite hobby _____

Each predicate needs a subject. Complete each sentence.
Add capital letters and end punctuation.

9. _____told me about Ellen

10. _____ put the saddle on the horses

11. _____ amused her for an hour

12. _____ went home

13. _____ was famous at one time

14. _____ ran faster than ever before

# Adjectives
## Lesson 40

Have the lights come on?

- An **adjective** is a word that describes a noun or pronoun.

     The **tired young** boy rode his pony down the **dusty** road.

Write an adjective for each noun below.

1. doll _____
2. farm _____
3. apple _____
4. palace _____
5. machine _____
6. kangaroo _____
7. floor _____
8. paper _____
9. giraffe _____
10. hair _____
11. flower _____
12. sky _____
13. tree _____
14. sweater _____
15. fence _____
16. heart _____
17. bottle _____
18. piano _____
19. spider _____
20. smoke _____

21. bridge _____
22. kitten _____
23. sea _____
24. calf _____
25. mitten _____
26. tricycle _____
27. crown _____
28. corn _____
29. soap _____
30. storm _____
31. squirrel _____
32. girls _____
33. city _____
34. butter _____
35. pole _____
36. river _____
37. dress _____
38. volcano _____
39. doctor _____
40. dinosaur _____

# Adjectives

Lesson 41

Name _____

Date _____

- An adjective is a word that describes a noun or pronoun in three ways.

  An adjective tells **what kind:**
  The **fluffy yellow** duck looked for its mother.

  An adjective points out **which one:**
  **That** boy is in my class **this** year.

  An adjective tells **how many:**
  I'll give you **several** reasons why you must write **two** reports.

Circle the adjective(s) in each sentence.

1. Charlene picked red and yellow roses from her garden.

2. Those pupils passed their spelling test.

3. This man is our new teacher.

4. Both children attended the birthday party.

5. My parents are busy people.

6. Spot is a playful, frisky dog.

7. Please sharpen these pencils, Frank.

8. Rudy hit two home runs in that game.

9. Judy bought two peaches and one red apple.

10. My kite glided through the bright blue sky.

11. Ira moved to a small town in Montana.

12. There are twelve boys and fourteen girls in Kit's class.

13. Tammy read her book under the shady elm tree.

14. Linda put on both mittens before going out to play in the soft new snow.

15. Those birds ate every sweet berry off my plants.

Go!
Go!
Go!

# Adverbs

## Lesson 42

- An **adverb** is a word that usually describes a verb.
  It can also describe an adjective or other adverb.

> An adverb tells **how:**
> The boys ran **fast.**
>
> An adverb tells **when:**
> Dinner will be ready at **five o'clock.**
>
> An adverb tells **where:**
> Joshua played **nearby.**
>
> An adverb tells **how often:**
> Julie takes dance lessons **daily.**

Does the adverb in bold type tell **how, when, where,** or **how often?**

1. _____ Sue can **easily** finish the homework.

2. _____ We take a swim in our pool **daily.**

3. _____ The girls were **nearby**.

4. _____ It rained **yesterday.**

5. _____ The Browns don't live **here**.

6. _____ Were you hurt **badly**?

7. _____ Father spoke **firmly** to Jason and Henry.

8. _____ That speeding car appeared **suddenly.**

9. _____ Corrine ran **quickly** to the store.

10. _____ Paul came first and Jenny was **next.**

11. _____ My family goes out to dinner **once** a week.

12. _____ The first day of school is **tomorrow.**

13. _____ I **often** help my parents with the yardwork.

14. _____ The sparks seemed to fly **everywhere.**

15. _____ Peter and Deanna played **quietly.**

> It's just like ringing a bell. You're doing swell!

# Adverbs

## Lesson 43

- An **adverb** is a word that describes a verb, adjective, or other adverb. It usually tells **when, how, where,** or **how often** something is done.

Circle the adverb in each sentence.

1. Jerry behaved badly.

2. The rain fell gently.

3. I will surely pass the test.

4. The children sang happily.

5. The stream rushed by swiftly.

6. Francine came by early.

7. The stars glittered brightly.

8. The neighbors' dog barked loudly.

9. Mr. Ito drove carefully.

10. Tim finally arrived.

11. The kitten purred quietly.

12. Joey and I often go to the movies.

13. The baseball game is over now.

14. Alice is leaving tomorrow.

15. He drove by hurriedly.

16. Sherri walked rapidly.

17. The next town is not far.

18. Bobby quietly watched television.

19. Corby won the race easily.

20. The chilly, winter wind blew strongly.

Nothing can stop you once you know how!

# Adjectives and Adverbs

**Name** _____

## Lesson 44

**Date** _____

*It's fun to watch you work!*

- An **adjective** is a word that describes a person, place, or thing by telling **what kind**, **which one**, or **how many**.

- An **adverb** is a word that describes a verb, adjective, or other adverb by telling **how, when, where,** or **how often** something is done.

Tell whether the word in bold type is an **adjective** or an **adverb**.

1. **both** puppies _____
2. **blue** sky _____
3. ran **quickly** _____
4. **bad** report _____
5. finish **easily** _____
6. **soft** blanket _____
7. **often** help _____
8. **green** grass _____
9. **large** house _____
10. **black** clouds _____
11. **sweet** oranges _____
12. **sticky** glue _____
13. flew **high** _____
14. swam **yesterday** _____
15. **yellow** daisy _____
16. **broken** dish _____
17. ended **suddenly** _____
18. blew **strongly** _____
19. **pretty** girl _____
20. **cold** drink _____

21. **that** tree _____
22. played **quietly** _____
23. **happy** children _____
24. were **nearby** _____
25. **bright** sun _____
26. worked **merrily** _____
27. **fuzzy** slippers _____
28. **badly** hurt _____
29. flashed **brightly** _____
30. **colorful** shirt _____
31. walked **slowly** _____
32. **brown** spots _____
33. **tiny** fly _____
34. jumped **quickly** _____
35. **hot** water _____
36. **timid** cat _____
37. came **here** _____
38. barked **loudly** _____
39. **clear** lake _____
40. **happily** sang _____

# Business Letters

## Lesson 45

That's it! Keep it up!

The six parts to a business letter are the **heading, inside address, greeting** or **salutation, body, closing,** and **signature**.

1. The heading is the address of the person who wrote the letter and the date.

2. The inside address is the name and address of the company to whom the letter is written. Each important word of the company's name begins with a capital letter.

3. The greeting or salutation is the way the writer says hello. Use a colon after the greeting.

4. The body is what is written to the company.

5. The closing is the way the writer says good-bye. The closing always begins with a capital letter and ends with a comma.

6. The signature is the name of the person who wrote the letter.

The six parts to a business letter are.

1. _____ , 2. _____ , 3. _____ ,

4. _____ , 5. _____ , and 6. _____ ,

Identify the six parts to a business letter on the correct lines.

7. _____ 207 Hope Street
Alpine, Oregon 97408
June 10, 1981

Creative Crafts  8. _____
64 Seventh Street
New York, New York 10022

Dear Sir:  9. _____

   I would like to order one Creative Craft Kit.  I have enclosed a money order for five dollars and seventy-five cents.  10. _____

11. _____ Sincerely yours,

12. _____ Allan Baynes

# Review Test 4

Draw two lines under each verb. Some sentences have a helping verb.
Circle each helping verb.

1. Each child read a poem.

2. Janet may come to my house.

3. I am twelve years old.

4. The children were at the party.

5. Pete baked cookies today.

6. He has eaten all the cookies.

7. Leslie and Tina are walking home today.

Draw one line under the complete subject.
Draw two lines under the complete predicate.

8. Aunt Annie will visit us next week.

9. Basketball and tennis are my favorite sports.

10. The glass of milk spilled on the counter.

Circle each adjective.

11. That girl won the race.

12. Danny wore a heavy, blue jacket.

13. Becky ordered three hamburgers.

Circle each adverb.

14. They played the music quietly.

15. I often jog to school.

16. Larry swam here.

17. Fred worked busily.

The six parts of a business letter are:

18. _____ , 19. _____ , 20. _____ ,

21. _____ , 22. _____ , and 23. _____

24. What punctuation mark comes after the greeting in a
    business letter? _____

Name _____

Date _____

Remember the rules!

Circle the first letter of each word that should begin with a capital letter. Put periods, exclamation points, and question marks in the right places.

1. who invented the airplane

2. there were many people interested in airplanes

3. on december 17, 1903, orville and wilbur wright flew their airplane

4. what an exciting event

5. they must have had a wonderful christmas

6. where did orville and wilbur live

7. orville and wilbur lived in dayton, ohio

8. a man from france, alberto santos-dumot, made flights of several hundred feet in 1906

9. the french airplanes differed from the american planes

10. the germans soon built a lighter and more powerful plane

11. did glenn h curtiss build the hydro-airplane and flying boat

12. great grandma and grandpa have many memories of the early airplanes

13. have you seen your great grandparents, dr and mrs wicker recently

14. they came to our home on monday, november 3

15. "do you want to hear about the jet-propelled planes" great grandpa asked

16. he continued, "many of these planes had supersonic speed"

17. "when was the first nonstop flight across the atlantic ocean" i asked

18. "the english aviators, alcock and brown, flew from newfoundland to ireland in about 16 hours in the year 1919," answered great grandma

19. "that's fantastic" i replied

20. great grandma and grandpa promised to tell me about airships during their thanksgiving visit

# Punctuation Review
## Lesson 47

Think and remember.

Name _____

Date _____

Put in commas, apostrophes, quotation marks, and underlining in the right places.

1. Charlene read the book Sea Turtles last month.

2. When she finished the book, she wrote a story called
   Turtles, Turtles, and More Turtles!

3. What types of turtles did you read about? asked Valerie.

4. I read about the leatherback the loggerhead the hawksbill and the
   green turtle she replied.

5. A leatherbacks weight can be between 800 and 1200 pounds said Charlene.

6. I don't believe it! exclaimed Valerie.

7. Valerie its true replied Charlene.

8. The loggerhead is also amazing Valerie said Charlene.

9. Charlene continued The female can sometimes lay 1000 eggs!

10. Have you Charlene ever seen one? asked Valerie.

11. No I havent said Charlene. But, my grandmother saw one near Miami Florida.

12. Oh when did she see it Charlene? asked Valerie.

13. Here is my grandmothers letter said Charlene.

14.                                                    10 Hancock Avenue
15.                                                    Miami Florida
16.                                                    March 18 1998

17. Dear Charlene

18. Are you still studying turtles? Im sending a photo of an amazing sight.
    Its a loggerhead turtle. It weighs about 400 pounds.

19.                                                    Love

20.                                                    Grandma Kate

21. Charlene walked to Valeries house.

22. Would you like to see the pennies nickels and dimes Im
    collecting? asked Valerie.

# Sentence and Word Usage Review

Name _____

Date _____

## Lesson 48

Change each sentence fragment to a complete sentence.
Change the run-on sentences to good sentences.
Remember to use capital letters and punctuation.

1. my friend and i _____

   _____

2. saw it coming _____

   _____

3. she ate dinner, it was tasty _____

   _____

4. the test was easy, i studied this time _____

   _____

Change each singular noun to its plural form.

5. church_____   6. berry _____   7. toy _____

8. man_____   9. knife _____   10. piano _____

11. boy _____   12. ax_____   13. cake_____

Fill in the blanks.

14. _____ **(There, Their, They're)** jumping

    _____ **(off, off of)** the bridge.

15. The children _____ **(sit, set)** the books on _____
    **(there, their, they're)** desks.

16. I don't have _____ **(no, any)** time to pick up the _____
    **(to, too, two)** children.

17. Please _____ **(sit, set)** over _____.
    **(there, their, they're)**

18. He _____ **(may, can)** run _____. **(well, good)**

19. I bought apples _____ **(off, off of, from)** the grocer
    _____ **(to, too, two)** make an apple pie.

20. _____ **(May, Can)** I have a cup _____ **(off, of)** milk?

21. _____ **(There, Their, They're)** _____ **(well,
    good)** workers, _____. **(to, too, two)**

22. He hasn't _____ **(nothing, anything)** left.

# Noun and Verb Review

## Lesson 49

Name _____

Date _____

Circle each noun.

1. Eddie and Tori caught three fish in Legg Lake.

2. My birthday is this Saturday.

3. The horses seem tired.

4. We are leaving Idaho on November 25.

5. Mother is feeding the baby.

6. Linda, please set the table.

7. The policeman helped that little boy.

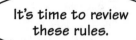

It's time to review these rules.

Circle each common noun. Draw a line under each proper noun.

8. Joe and Jenny will visit the Grand Canyon this summer.

9. Paul and Irene are taking the family to Sea World.

10. Have the children been to the San Diego Zoo?

11. The children played tag in their backyard.

12. Mrs. Langford traveled to West Virginia.

13. Did Mom leave for the office yet?

14. My parents took a cruise to Mexico.

Draw two lines under each verb. Circle each helping verb.

15. The children appear happy.

16. Patty is wearing a new dress.

17. Those are my best shoes.

18. Mary completed her homework.

19. Ginger looks tired.

20. Mother baked two chocolate cakes.

21. Andy has broken five plates.

# Pronoun Review
## Lesson 50

Name _____

Date _____

Circle each pronoun.

1. Our family is having its tenth annual reunion.

2. Will you be able to come?

3. We will have many good things to eat.

4. I helped Mom bake three pies.

5. I am also going to make a potato salad.

6. My cousin, Jim, is going to bring fried chicken.

7. He is going to fry it himself.

8. Aunt Louise and Uncle Wes are bringing their famous barbecued ribs.

9. They always use their special homemade sauce.

10. Here they come now!

11. It is Grandma and Grandpa.

12. Who did they bring with them?

13. My Aunt Sally is in their car!

14. She is my favorite aunt.

15. I see cousin Kathy and her little girl.

16. It looks as if she brought a baked ham.

17. We are going to have a feast.

18. Twenty-seven people will be at our party.

19. We will all sit in my backyard.

20. What will they sit on?

21. They all brought folding chairs.

22. Mom and I are going to bring out the food.

23. Dad is bringing out his camera.

24. Can you join us?

# Adjective Review

## Lesson 51

Name _____

Date _____

Circle each adjective.

1. The furry cat scurried up the giant palm tree.

2. What an enormous pizza!

3. Mom's fragrant perfume filled the air.

4. Glenda used chunky peanut butter for her sandwich.

5. The tall basketball player took a long hot shower.

6. That is the highest mountain I've ever seen.

7. Rachel slipped on the wet floor.

8. I squeezed five sour lemons.

9. Lenny bought one dozen large eggs.

10. Francine wore tiny pearl earrings.

It's worth all the effort!

11. The strong wind blew dry leaves all over the street.

12. Grandma received a blue coat for her birthday.

13. That boy ran a great race.

14. Our new orchestra played loudly.

15. Use the roughest sandpaper you can find.

16. Are you going to wear your new brown shoes?

17. Put the dirty clothes in the yellow basket.

18. Dorene added a lace collar to her pale blue dress.

19. Liz chews sugarless gum.

20. Mrs. McAlister went to buy three small apples and two bananas.

21. The children poured water over the dry sand.

22. Do you know my Uncle Sam?

23. Cybil is a cheerful student.

24. Do you know any mean or greedy people?

# Adverb Review

## Lesson 52

Name _____

Date _____

Circle each adverb.

Nothing can stop you once you know how!

1. The animal was badly hurt.

2. My friends came here.

3. Mike's kite flew high.

4. The thunderstorm ended suddenly.

5. My friends and I went swimming yesterday.

6. That snail slowly chewed the leaves.

7. We happily sang a birthday song.

8. I will gladly tell you about our vacation.

9. School is now over.

10. Does your aunt live nearby?

11. Jason sat quietly in his room.

12. Tammy gently stroked Fluffy's fur.

13. The movie finally ended.

14. Maureen hurriedly completed her chores.

15. That beautiful butterfly glided gently through the air.

16. The neon signs flashed brightly.

17. I climbed slowly up the hillside.

18. The sun shone brightly over Clear Lake.

19. Henry proudly showed us his awards.

20. We quickly ate dinner.

21. The baby cried loudly.

22. William carefully washed the dishes.

# Subject and Predicate Review
## Lesson 53

Name _____

Date _____

Draw one line under the complete subject.
Draw two lines under the complete predicate.

That's it!
Keep it up!

1. Sandra and Allen went for a walk.

2. They walked along the seashore.

3. Allen picked up a variety of shells.

4. The friends studied the hermit crabs.

5. They also saw sea stars and sea urchins.

6. The sea cucumber is a strange animal.

7. They had never seen so many different sea creatures.

8. The tide pool area along the seashore is a very interesting place.

9. Allen decided to go for a swim.

10. He gives the shells to Sandra.

11. Sandra asks Allen to wait for her.

12. The waves are becoming stronger.

13. The lifeguards put out red flags.

14. Allen and Sandra decide to stay out of the water.

15. The friends collect buckets, cups, and spoons.

16. They will build a sand monster.

17. The huge sand monster attracts many people.

18. Soon, many sand monsters appear along the sandy beach.

19. Sandra and Allen are very proud of their creation.

20. All the sand monsters are unusual.

21. Their sand monster was the funniest.

22. Some of the sand monsters were over seven feet long.

23. Other sand monsters were very tall.

24. The friends will come to the beach again tomorrow.

# Capitalization Test

## Lesson 54

Name _____

Date _____

Circle the first letter of each word that should begin with a capital letter.

Think and remember!

1. jesse and gina took fluffy to danboro park.

2. aunt paula is my mother's sister.

3. professor barton will speak to our class on monday.

4. did you see dr. swift in april?

5. i sent mother and father a card on valentine's day.

6. my family and i had a picnic at big bear lake.

7. one of my favorite books is little women by louisa may alcott.

8. aunt sophie sent the boys special gifts from ireland.

9. jackie asked, "when will we leave?"

10. have you tasted the french pastry mother brought home?

11. the chorus sang "america the beautiful" during the school assembly.

12. "what a great day!" exclaimed captain andrews.

13. when is columbus day?

14. "may i have a few chocolate chip cookies?" asked tim.

15. i read "hansel and gretel" to my nephew.

16. "i can speak english, french, and spanish," said maria.

17. when did judge r.j. mason come to your house?

18. the title of edna's report is "the people of india".

19. my youngest cousin was born on friday, january 22, 1999.

20. mr. and mrs. gomez live in the new green house on cherry avenue.

# Punctuation Test

## Lesson 55

Name _____

Date _____

Put in periods, commas, apostrophes, quotation marks, underlining, question marks, and exclamation points in the right places.

1. Mrs Ryan read the story Peter Pan to her young class

2. Did the children enjoy it

3. Yes they all loved it

4. Will you read the story again asked Brian

5. Mrs Ryan answered Well I will read it again before the end of the day

6. Its music time children announced Mrs Ryan

7. The children sang Pop Goes the Weasel

8. After music time, the children took a long rest

9. Brian Lisa and Henry were the class monitors

10. The children picked up the straws milk and crackers from the cafeteria

11. Henry will you pass out the milk asked Mrs Ryan

12. Lisa and Brian passed out the straws and crackers

13. Lets hear the story again said J P Carlin

14. After school, Brian Patsy and Darrel walked home together

15. Darrel did you live in Grovedale Washington before moving to Centerville Montana asked Patsy

16. Yes replied Darrel

17. We moved here in October 1998 he continued

18. Oh thats why you didnt start school until October 12 1998 said Patsy

19. Theres Anns house shouted Brian

20. Thats my best friends house said Patsy

21. Whos your best friend asked Darrel

22. Terry M Meyers is my best friend she replied

You're going to make it!

# Sentence and Word Usage Test

## Lesson 56

Fill in the blanks.

1. We don't have _____ **(no, any)** milk or cereal.

2. Margie borrowed a cup _____ **(of, off)** sugar _____ **(off, off of, from)** Louise.

3. _____ **(They're, There, Their)** meeting _____ **(they're, there, their)** parents over _____. **(they're, there, their)**

4. _____ **(May, Can)** you come _____ **(to, two, too)** my performance at _____ o'clock? **(to, two, too)**

5. She did that job _____. **(good, well)**

6. Barry ought to _____ **(of, have)** been _____. **(they're, there, their)**

7. The children will _____ **(sit, set)** on the large cushions.

8. Jenny doesn't have _____ **(no, a)** bicycle.

Change each noun to its possessive form.

9. child _____   10. princess _____   11. mother_____

12. boy _____   13. poems_____   14. lamb _____

15. mice _____   16. tomatoes _____   17. nurses_____

18. enemies_____   19. lady _____   20. men_____

Write **S** before each line that is a good sentence.
Write **F** before each line that is a fragment.
Write **RO** before each line that is a run-on.

21. _____ Wanda rides the bus home every day.

22. _____ My best friend at the library.

23. _____ Will meet them at school.

24. _____ They played in the pool, it was a hot day.

Be patient! You're doing great!

# Parts of Speech Test

**Lesson 57**

Name _____

Date _____

Write a proper noun for each common noun.
Write a common noun for each proper noun.

1. country _____    2. boy _____

3. lake _____    4. California _____

5. France _____    6. Granger Park _____

7. Sally _____    8. street _____

Draw a line under each noun. Circle each pronoun.

9. Yolanda walked her sister to school.

10. Karen and I played volleyball with our friends.

11. My father and Uncle Ken attended their club meeting.

12. Toby made a new dress.

Draw two lines under each verb. Circle each helping verb.

13. Randy and Father are planting corn seeds.

14. The rain is falling gently on the window.

15. Who was that young man?

Draw one line under the complete subject.
Draw two lines under the complete predicate.

16. Sammy and Katie watched a football game on television.

17. My family and I enjoy homemade ice cream for dessert.

18. Elsa is visiting Barbara this afternoon.

Tell whether the word in heavy type is an adjective or an adverb.

19. **enormous** bear _____    20. **pink** roses _____

21. **sour** lemons _____    22. reads **quietly** _____

23. pounded **strongly** _____    24. **three** books _____

25. was **here** _____    26. **old** tree _____

 FS123254 Skill Drill Grammar Grades 3–4

# Skill Drill Grammar Answers

**Page 2**
1. Sue  2. She; Aunt; Irene; Monday  3. Cousin; Billy; Cousin; Corrine  4. Aunt; Irene; Culver City; California; April  5. To; Sue  6. She; Orange Grove Avenue; Grovedale High School  7. Sue; Billy; Corrine  8. Aunt Irene; Sue; Saturday; Sunday  9. They; Palm Park; Saturday  10. Sue; Santa Monica Beach; Sunday  11. Dear; Sue; Thank; Billy; Corrine; You; I; Independence Day; July; Love; Aunt Irene.

**Page 3**
1. Who; Island; Blue; Dolphins; Mr. Brown  2. Valerie; I  3. Mr. Brown; The; <u>Treasure Island</u>  4. The; Mrs. Veirling  5. I; Miss Francine Orloff; Miss Tammy Wynters; Mrs. Vierling  6. Mrs. Orloff; Mrs. Wynters  7. Tammy; Dr. Adams; Mrs. Wynters  8. We; Professor Egan; Virginia; Francine  9. Just; Greg Neiman  10. Mr. Brown; Greg.

**Page 4**
1. ?  2. !  3. J.T.; .  4. Ms.; Ave.; .  5. !  6. Dr.; T.; .  7. ?  8. ?

**Page 5**
Numbers 1, 3, 6, 7, 8, 11, 14, and 16 are sentences. The remainder are fragments.

**Page 6**
Numbers 3, 5, 8, and 9 are sentences. The remainder are run-on sentences.

**Page 7**
1. Independence,  2. October 10,  3. December 15,  4. Jarvis,; Kentucky,; December,  5. Blocher,; Indiana,; December 17,  6. December 21,; Jarvis  7. Canton,  8. Canton,; Ohio,; December 24,  9. No commas  10. No comma  11. Grandma,; December 17,; Love.,

**Page 8**
1. Doug,; John,  2. Oh,  3. swam, ate lunch,  4. Well,  5. Doug, John,  6. Oh,  7. floating, paddling,  8. Leo,  9. hamburgers, drinks,  10. Who, Leo,  11. Well,  12. Yes, hamburgers, fries,

**Page 9**
1. may  2. may; too  3. leave, two  4. sits  5. good  6. to  7. may  8. set  9. sit  10. can; well  11. let  12. good  13. can; well  14. can; good; well.

**Page 10**
1. anything  2. any  3. anything  4. anyone  5. anything  6. ever  7. any  8. anyone  9. anything  10. a  11. a  12. any  13. ever  14. anything  15. anyone  16. a  17. any  18. anything

**Page 11**
Numbers 1, 2, 4, 5, 6, 9, 10, 12, 14, 15, 16, 17, 18, 19, 23, 25, 27, and 28 end in s. Numbers 3, 7, 8, 11, 13, 20, and 26 end in es. Number 21 is children. Number 22 is geese. Number 24 is men.

**Page 12**
Numbers 5, 9, 10, 12, 17, 20, 23, 25, and 28 end in s. For the remaining words change the y to i and add es.

**Page 13**
1. My; Mrs. Rincoff; Ireland  2. Connie; May; I; Grandma; Friday  3. Mr. T Parker; Whittier; California  4. We; Yellowstone National Park; July  5. How; Professor Newcomb  6. !  7. Dr. H.; .; 8. Ms.; ?  9-10. teacher judgement  11. Carrie,  12. Yes,; Los Angeles,; California,; May,;  13. salad,; pizza,  14. any  15. well  16. sit  17. lunches  18. cherries  19. calves  20. rays  21. docks  22. boxes.

**Page 14**
1. Europe; Asia  2. China  3. Chinese  4. Chinese  5. India; Turkey  6. Turkish  7. Indians  8. Turkish  9. Turkish; French: France  10. French; Chinese  11. Europe  12. Sweden  13. Swedish; English  14. Spain; Spanish.

**Page 15**
1. There Are Rocks in My Socks  2. Gus Was a Friendly Ghost  3. The Book of Giant Stories  4. The Teeny, Tiny Witches  5. Exploring the World of Fossils  6. The World of Insects  7. Trilobite, Dinosaur, and Man  8. The Arts of Walt Disney  9. The Life and Times of Eight Presidents  10. Children Around the World  11. Nature's Wonderful Family  12. The Pilgrims and Their Times  13. At the Seaside  14. To Father  15. Star-Spangled Banner  16. Yellow Rose of Texas  17. The New Family  18. Sleeping Beauty

**Page 16**
1. "Hearts Were Made to Give Away"  2. "A Room of Her Own"  3. The Stars and Stripes Forever  4. "Blue Belts of Scotland"  5. "Silent Night"  6. Twinkle, Twinkle, Little Star  7. "Bump"  8. "Making a Dirt House"  9. "America the Beautiful"  10. "Chad and the Toy Monkey"  11. "Sleeping Beauty"  12. Paul Revere's Ride  13. "Three Blind Mice"  14. Home on the Range

**Page 17**
Titles in all 16 sentences should be underlined.  1. Wishes and Christmas Wishes  2. A Free Nation  3. America Indians  4. The Frog and the Toad  5. The Name Game  6. Fascinating Facts  7. Cinderella  8. Little Women  9. Me and My Little Brain  10. The Mouse and the Motorcycle  11. Grapes of Wrath  12. Shadow of the Bull  13. My Friend Flicka  14. 20,000 Leagues Under the Sea  15. The Rule Book  16. The Hardy Boys

**Page 18**
Numbers 1 and 4 are I. Q. Numbers 2 and 3 are D. Q.  5-9. Teacher judgment.

**Page 19**
Begin the first word in each sentence with a capital letter except numbers 7 and 9. Number 7: I;  Number 9: Do

**Page 20**
1. "What - !"  2. "Sam – swimming?"  3. "That – idea!"  4. "I need,"; "to – towel,"  5. "Let's – pond,"  6. "Do – Park?"  7. "I'm – idea."  8. "Why not?"  9. "I've – unsafe,"  10. "Well,"; "maybe – right."  11. "This – swim,"  12. "Okay,"; "let's – in!"  13. "The – great!"  14. "We'll – tomorrow."

**Page 21**
1. reading?; Mark.  2. facts,"; David.  3. asked,; river?"  4. River,"; Mark.  5. asked,; highest?"  6. book,"; David,; highest,"  7. eggs?"; David.  8. Australia,"; Mark.  9. other?" asked.  10. Australia,"; David.  11. webs?"; David.  12. Sure,"; Mark.  13. food,"; David.  14. leaves,"; Mark.  15. right,"; David.

**Page 22**
1. cake!  2. it?  3. replied,  4. Jenna?  5. replied,  6. continued,  7. said,  8. said,  9. club!"  10. said,  11. Wednesday?'  12. then,"  13. Friday,"  14. Thursday?"  15. desserts,"; Dennis,

**Page 23**
1. Sir  2. Larry  3. Karen  4. Jim  5. Mom  6. young man  7. Dad  8. Frank  9. Miss Franklin  10. son  11. Dorene  12. Julie  13. Miss  14. Coach  15. Mom  16. Robert  17. Dr. Elliott  18. Mike

**Page 24**
1. Curtis  2. ,Ralph  3. ,Curtis  4. ,Ralph,  5. ,Gloria  6. Vera,  7. ,Curtis  8. ,Vera  9. Vera,  10. ,Gloria  11. ,Vera  12. Children,  13. ,Mother,  14. Ralph,  15. ,Ralph,

**Page 25**
1. My; Ireland  2. The Irish  3. Do; Irish; Scottish  4. <u>Land of the Midnight Sun</u>  5. "Yellow Submarine"  6. "Home on the Range"  7. "Our Trip to Hawaii".  8. <u>Magicians</u>  9. "Are - School?"; Kim,  10. "No,"; Micky, "we - trip,"  11. , "Where - going?"  12. "We're - States,"; Micky.  13. "That - exciting!"; Kim.  14. Davey,  15. ,Sarah,  16. arrives, Davey

**Page 26**
1. their  2. They're  3. There  4. there; their  5. They're  6. their  7. There  8. their; their  9. They're; their  10. their

**Page 27**
1. of  2. off  3. from  4. have  5. have  6. off  7. from  8. of

**Page 28**
1. Soccer; sport; country  2. Lorenzo; soccer  3. Lorenzo; Aztecs  4. Aztecs; team; Los Angeles  5. Lorenzo; soccer; Walnut Chargers  6. friends; team  7. Chargers; league; championship; year  8. Lorenzo; team; title  9-16. teacher judgment

**Page 29**
(pronouns are underlined)  1. Rebecca, class, <u>her</u>, Africa  2. half, <u>it</u>, dessert  3. Rebecca, <u>you</u>, name, dessert, world, Mrs. Campo  4. <u>I</u>; <u>it</u>, Sahara Desert  5. <u>It</u>, grassland, forests, <u>her</u>  6. <u>they</u>, part, Africa, equator, Mike  7. <u>You</u>, Mike, Mrs. Campo  8. <u>she</u>, farmers, huts, tents  9. Africans, buildings, <u>we</u>, <u>our</u>, country, Patsy  10. <u>they</u>, Mrs. Campo  11. <u>Their</u>, country, <u>ours</u>, Rebecca  12. <u>we</u>, deal, <u>their</u>, country, Mrs. Campo  13. part, world, <u>we</u>  14. <u>Our</u>, class, Asia, <u>she</u>

**Page 30**
Numbers 1, 2, 5, 8, 11, 12, 14, 18, 20, 24, 28, and 29 end in s. Numbers 3, 4, 7, 10, 13, 15, 22, 26, and 27 end in es. Numbers 6, 16, 19, and 25 change the y to i and add es. Number 9 leaves.  Number 17 mice. Number 21 calves. Number 23 women. Number 30 loaves.

**Page 31**
All numbers end in 's.

**Page 32**
Numbers 4, 11, 31, and 34 end in 's. All others end with an ' after the s.

**Page 33**
1. sister/c; England/p; August/p  2. Mr. Ching/p; principal/c; Olive School/p  3. Ken/p; player/c  4. Dallas Cowboys/p  5. Canada/p; United States of America/p  6. Mrs. Noce/p; house/c; Lanigon Street/p  7. food/c  8. Sandy/p; exams/c English/p;  9. Tony/p  10. team/c, Raiders/p  11. Mr. and Mrs. Thatcher/p; Daytona Beach/p  12. President/p; United States/p; White House/p  13. Gilda/p; Goldie/p; goldfish/c  14. Greg/p; Penn Park/p; Saturday/p  15. flight/c; Kentucky/p; hours/c

**Page 34**
Teacher judgment

**Page 35**
Teacher judgment

**Page 36**
**Paragraph 1:** afternoon./part./So/Nancy. The/lines. Nancy/well. It/turn. How/do?/well. The/Friday.
**Paragraph 2:** The/arrived. Today/Friday./board. Both/part. They/time. Barbara/part. They/disappointed. Then/again. Both/play./indeed.

# Skill Drill Grammar Answers

**Page 37**
1. there 2. off; 3. They're 4. their 5. have 6. from 7. My – pronoun; family - noun; I – pronoun; Alabama – noun 8. We – pronoun; shoes – noun 9. Karen – noun; her – pronoun; house – noun 10-13. teacher judgment 14. child's; 15. houses' 16. man's 17. tree's 18. books' 19. women's 20. RO 21. S 22. F

**Page 38**
1. answered 2. jumped 3. asked 4. mailed 5. barked 6. marched 7. ate 8. buzzed 9. kissed 10. camped 11. packed 12. chased 13. read 14. emptied 15. hopped 16. vacationed 17. whistled 18. shut 19. scratched 20. pulled

**Page 39**
1. has delivered 2. were building 3. was knocking 4. are leaving 5. is cooking 6. have eaten 7. can swim 8. am sewing 9. may walk 10. have arrived 11. did complete 12. do answer 13. has thrown 14. is working

**Page 40**
1. was 2. are 3. am 4. became 5. were 6. is 7. appear 8. remained 9. looked 10. seems 11. is 12. are 13. am 14. were

**Page 41**
1. Irene, Melissa, store – nouns; are going – verbs 2. apples, supermarket – nouns; looked – verb 3. friend, David, Manchester Junior High School – nouns; attends – verb 4. Fluff, butterfly – nouns; is chasing – verbs 5. Sandy, movies – nouns; remained – verb 6. Ira – noun; feels – verb 7. Dorene, marshmallows, campfire – nouns; toasted – verb 8. Marianne, party - nouns; has planned – verbs 9. Erin – noun; seemed – verb 10. Maggie, Lisa, feet, parade – nouns; had – verb 11. Pete - noun; Josh- noun; home – noun; are going – verbs 12. Uncle John, fish – nouns; caught – verb

**Page 42**
subjects are: 1. The hunter 2. The two groups of children 3. Carrie 4. The fierce dog 5. My sister 6. Leslie 7. The boys 8. Mrs. Kemper 9. David 10. Vera and Yolanda 11. Meg, Amy, and Beth 12. Lloyd 13. Father 14. Tony 15. Mom, Dad, and I

**Page 43**
Teacher judgment

**Page 44**
Teacher judgment

**Page 45**
1. red; yellow, her 2. Those; their; spelling 3. This; new 4. Both; birthday 5. My; busy 6. playful; frisky 7. these 8. two; that 9. two; one; red 10. My, bright; blue 11. small 12. twelve; fourteen 13. her; shady; elm 14. both; new; soft 15. Those; every; sweet; my

**Page 46**
1. how 2. how often 3. where 4. when 5. where 6. how 7. how 8. when 9. how 10. when 11. how often 12. when 13. how often 14. where 15. how

**Page 47**
1. badly 2. gently 3. surely 4. happily 5. swiftly 6. early 7. brightly 8. loudly 9. carefully 10. finally 11. quietly 12. often 13. now 14. tomorrow 15. hurriedly 16. rapidly 17. far 18. quietly 19. easily 20. strongly

**Page 48**
Numbers 3, 5, 7, 13, 14, 17, 18, 22, 24, 26, 28, 29, 31, 34, 37, 38, and 40 are adverbs. The remaining numbers are adjectives.

**Page 49**
1. heading 2. inside address 3. greeting 4. body 5. closing 6. signature 7. heading 8. inside address 9. greeting 10. body 11. closing 12. signature

**Part 50**
1. read 2. may come 3. am 4. were 5. baked 6. has eaten 7. are walking 8. Aunt Annie - subject; will visit us next week. - predicate 9. Basketball and tennis - subject; are my favorite sports - predicate 10. The glass of milk - subject; spilled on the counter - predicate 11. That 12. heavy; blue 13. three 14. quietly 15. often 16. here 17. busily 18. heading 19. inside address 20. greeting 21. body 22. closing 23. signature 24. colon

**Page 51**
1. Who; ? 2. There; . 3. On; December; Orville; Wilbur; Wright; . 4. What; ! 5. They; Christmas; . 6. Where; Orville; Wilbur; ? 7. Orville; Wilbur; Dayton; Ohio. 8. A; France; Alberto; Santos – Dumont; . 9. The; French; American; . 10. The; Germans; . 11. Did; Glenn; H.; Curtiss; ? 12. Great; Grandma; Grandpa; . 13. Have; Dr.; Mrs. Wicker; ? 14. They; Monday; November; . 15. "Do; ?; Great; Grandpa; . 16. He; Many; . 17. When; ?; I; . 18. The; English; Alcock; Brown; Newfoundland; Ireland; Great; Grandma; .19. That's; I; I 20. Great; Grandma; Grandpa; Thanksgiving; .

**Page 52**
1. underline Sea Turtles 2. "Turtles – Turtles!" 3. "What – about?" 4. "I read about the leatherback, the loggerhead, the hawksbill, and the green turtle," she replied. 5. "A leatherback's – pounds," 6. "I don't – it!" 7. "Valerie, it's true," 8. "The – amazing, Valerie," 9. continued, "The – eggs!" 10. "Have you, Charlene – one?" 11. "No, I haven't," said Charlene. "But, – Miami, Florida," 12. "Oh, - it, 13. "Here is my grandmother's letter," 15. Miami, Florida 16. March 18, 17. Dear Charlene, 18. I'm/It's 19. Love, 21. Valerie's 22. "Would you, Charlene – pennies, nickels, – I'm collecting?"

**Page 53**
1-4. Teacher judgment 5. churches 6. berries 7. toys 8. men 9. knives 10. pianos 11. boys 12. axes 13. lakes 14. They're; off 15. set; their 16. any; two 17. sit; there 18. can; well 19. from; to 20. may; of 21. They're; good; too 22. anything

**Page 54**
1. Eddie; Tori; fish; Legg Lake 2. birthday; Saturday 3. horses 4. Idaho; November 5. Mother; baby 6. Linda; table 7. policeman; boy (All capitalized words are proper nouns): 8. Joe; Jenny; Grand Canyon; summer 9. Paul; Irene; family; Sea World 10. children; San Diego Zoo 11. children; tag; backyard 12. Mrs. Langford; West Virginia 13. Mom; office 14. parents; cruise; Mexico 15. appear 16. is – helper; wearing 17. are 18. completed 19. looks 20. baked 21. has – helper; broken

**Page 55**
1. Our; its 2. you 3. we 4. I 5. I 6. My 7. He; it; himself 8. their 9. They; their 10. they 11. It 12. They; them 13. My; Their 14. She; my 15. I; her 16. It; she 17. We 18. our 19. We; my 20. they 21. They 22. I 23. his 24. you; us

**Page 56**
1. furry; giant; palm 2. enormous 3. fragrant 4. chunky 5. tall; basketball; long; hot 6. That; highest 7. wet 8. five; sour 9. one; dozen; large 10. tiny; pearl 11. strong; dry 12. blue 13. That; great 14. Our; new 15. roughest 16. new; brown 17. dirty; yellow 18. lace; pale; blue 19. sugarless 20. three; small; two 21. dry 22. my 23. cheerful 24. mean; greedy

**Page 57**
1. badly 2. here 3. high 4. suddenly 5. yesterday 6. slowly 7. happily 8. gladly 9. now; over 10. nearby 11. quietly 12. gently 13. finally 14. hurriedly 15. gently 16. brightly 17. slowly 18. brightly 19. proudly 20. quickly 21. loudly 22. carefully

**Page 58**
Subjects are: 1. Sandra and Allen 2. They 3. Allen 4. The friends 5. They 6. The sea cucumber 7. They 8. The tide pool area along the seashore 9. Allen 10. He 11. Sandra 12. The waves 13. The lifeguards 14. Allen and Sandra 15. The friends 16. They 17. The huge sand monster 18. Many sand monsters 19. Sandra and Allen 20. All the sand monsters 21. Their sand monster 22. Some of the sand monsters 23. Other sand monsters 24. The friends

**Page 59**
1. Jesse; Gina; Fluffy; Danboro Park 2. Aunt Paula 3. Professor Barton; Monday 4. Did; Dr. Swift; April 5. I; Mother; Father; Valentine's Day 6. My; I; Big Bear Lake 7. One: Little Women; Louise May Alcott 8. Aunt Sophie; Ireland 9. Jackie; When 10. Have; French; Mother 11. The; America; Beautiful 12. What; Captain; Andrews 13. When; Columbus Day 14. May; I; Tim 15. I; Hansel; Gretel 16. I; English; French; Spanish; Maria 17. When; Judge R. J. Mason 18. The; Edna's; The; People; India 19. My; Friday; January . 20. Mr.; Mrs. Gomez; Cherry Avenue

**Page 60**
1. Mrs.; "Peter Pan"; class. 2. it? 3. Yes., it. 4. "Will – again?"; Brian. 5. Mrs. Ryan answered, "Well, – day." 6. "It's; time,"; Mrs. Ryan. 7. "Pop Goes the Weasel." 8. rest. 9. Brian, Lisa,; monitors. 10. straws, milk,; cafeteria. 11. "Henry, – milk?"; Mrs. Ryan. 12. crackers. 13. "Let's – again,"; J. P. Carlin. 14. Brain, Patsy,; together. 15. "Darrel, – Grovedale, Washington,; Centerville, Montana?"; Patsy. 16. "Yes,"; Darrel. 17. "We – October, 1998,"; continued. 18. "Oh,; that's; didn't; October 12, 1998,"; Patsy. 19. "There's Ann's house!" shouted Brian. 20. "That's my best friend's house," said Patsy. 21. "Who's your best friend?" asked Darrel. 22. "Terry M. Meyers is my best friend," she replied.

**Page 61**
1. any 2. of; from 3. They're; their; there 4. Can; to; two 5. well 6. have; there 7. sit 8. a 9. child's 10. princess's 11. mother's 12. boy's 13. poems' 14. lamb's 15. mice's 16. tomatoes' 17. nurses' 18. enemies' 19. lady's 20. men's 21. S 22. F 23. F 24. RO

**Page 62**
1-8. Teacher judgment 9. Yolanda, sister, school – nouns; her – pronoun 10. Karen, volleyball, friends – nouns; I, our – pronouns 11. father, Uncle Ken, club meeting – nouns; My, their – pronouns 12. Toby, dress – nouns 13. are planting 14. is falling 15. was Subjects are: 16. Sammy and Katie 17. My family and I 18. Elsa Numbers 23, 25, and 22 are adverbs. Numbers 19, 21, 20, 24 and 26 are adjectives.

FS123254 Skill Drill Grammar Grades 3–4